Tales of the Chutzper Rebbe

A Selection From the Acidic Anthology

Rabbi Walter Rothschild

Illustrated by Paul Palnik

Alef Design Group

Tales of the Chutzper Rebbe

A Selection From the Acidic Anthology

ISBN# 1-881283-12-7

ALEF DESIGN GROUP · 4423 FRUITLAND AVENUE, LOS ANGELES, CA 90058
(800) 845–0662 · (213) 582-1200 · (213) 585–0327 FAX
E-MAIL misrad@torahaura.com

MANUFACTURED IN THE UNITED STATES OF AMERICA

The Chutzper Rebbe
talks with his Creator.
(They're best friends)

© Palnik 95

Foreword

Lost in the forests and plains of Eastern Europe lies
the little shtetl of Chutzp, the home of the Chutzper
dynasty of Chasidim. They have never head of
Martin Buber or Elie Wiesel, yet some-how their lives and stories
have an echo—a dark, reverse echo—of the Hasidic tales discovered
and told by those masters. Like the schlemiels of Chelm, the
Chutzper Chasidim somehow blunder their way through life, scat-
tering scraps of Jewish tradition as they go.

In this collection of what might be described as Mitnagdic or Anti-Hasidic tales some classic situations from 'Der Heym' are described from a Chutzper prespective. Whether in their travels, their work, their relationship to other Jews, to non-Jews or even to God, the Chutzper Hasidim are simple, literal and to the point— even if they are not always sure what the point is....

I was surprised to learn that no other scholarly work has been produced as yet on the Chutzper Chasidim; with luck, this present book should put back research on the topic by another decade or two.

This book will appeal most to those who know enough Chasidic stories and their backgrounds to be able to appreciate and enjoy the parodies of this genre. A full glossary is provides of all Hebrew or Yiddish terms used. The stories are improved—as all stories are—by telling them aloud and enjoying the style and language.

In presenting this work to a breathless audience, I should like to pay tribute to my family—who have put up with my many moods, ranging from heavy depression to deep despair as I have worked at the task of research, re-constitution and translation of these tales, sometimes combining fragments from a variety of sources. I can only hope that the effort has been worthwhile.

Rabbi Walter Rothschild
Leeds, November 1996

THE CHUTZPER REBBE... AS HE FINDS FAVOR WITH GOD AND MAN.

Table of Contents

11

The Prayer

It was told of the first Chutzper Rebbe (Reb Berel ben Shloime, or "The *RuBBiSH*") that at times when grief and trouble threatened the people of Israel, he would go into the forest, find a clearing, say a prayer and light a fire. And the trouble would be removed from the people of Israel.

12

The second Chutzper Rebbe (Reb Tovye ben Gershon, or "The *RaTBaG*"), at times when distress troubled the people of Israel, would also go into the forest. He could not find the clearing, but he would say the prayer and light the fire—and the trouble would be removed from the people of Israel.

The third Chutzper Rebbe, in a time of great drought and famine, also went into the forest. He couldn't find the clearing, and he did not know the prayer, but he could, and did, light the fire. When the forest stopped burning, three days later, he, too, had been removed from the people of Israel....

There is another version of the same story that the last Chutzper Rebbe used to say: "My great-grandfather knew not only the place to light the fire, but also how to light the fire and what to say. My grandfather knew the place and also how to light the fire, but not what to say. My father knew how to light the fire, but not the place, nor what to say. I myself know at least the story and how to light a fire when necessary. My Chasidim, though, cannot even find the matches, but are prepared to read all about it in American paperbacks."

The Holy Gatkes of Sliwowitz

One of the lesser-known disciples of the first Chutzper Rebbe was Reb Moshe of Sliwowitz. He was famous for his gatkes.

Every year, without fail, the pious Reb Moshe would wash his *gatkes*, not by taking them off (Heaven forbid!) but by wading, on Rosh ha-Shanah, into the waters of the River Prod during the *Tashlich* ceremony. "My sins are too ingrained," he would say, "just as are the crumbs in the pockets of my *gatkes*. So—just as I cannot scatter all the crumbs away, I must try to wash my sins away." As his disciples watched, he would wade into the stream and emerge with his *gatkes* changed from dark gray to light gray. Frequently he caught cold and had to spend Yom Kippur in his bed, drinking copious glasses of brandy mixed with hot water, but such is the price of piety. How the righteous suffer in this world! At least he had washed most of his sins away, and, he used to tell his disciples, "I am not worthy to have *all* the sins removed; only on the day of miracles, the day of full forgiveness, will my *gatkes* ever turn white again!"

Alas, one year the holy Reb Moshe decided to avoid catching cold by drinking copious glasses of brandy and hot water *before* entering the River Prod. It had been a wet autumn, and the river was running high. Before the horrified eyes of his Chasidim, Reb Moshe lost his footing, and was carried, struggling, downstream.

How appropriate were the words of the somber *Unetanneh Tokef* prayer that year! "Who shall live and who shall die...who by fire and who by water...on Rosh ha-Shanah it is decided, and on Yom

15

Kippur it is sealed...." It was not until two days had passed that Reb Moshe's lifeless body was pulled from the Prod, several miles downstream, by the outflow pipes of the Pamoliff Soap Factory.

Sadly, his Chasidim carried him back to Sliwowitz to prepare him for burial. But once there, they discovered a miracle had occurred! Reb Moshe's *gatkes*, holed and tattered by wear and battering against the rocks of the Prod, were sparkling white! The tzaddik had, indeed, gone to meet his Maker, sinless and in pure, clean underclothing!

In exultation at this miracle, it was decreed that it should be commemorated for all time to come. And this is the origin of the custom, observed in Sliwowitz to this very day, for the men to attend Yom Kippur services clad, not in white *kittels*, but in their *gatkes*, which are washed almost every year for this purpose. The womenfolk do not attend the shul on Yom Kippur, and the sight, we are told, has to be seen to be believed. Reb Moshe's original *gatkes* are now kept in a box on the *bimah* and taken out only during the *Musaf* prayers, and the highest praise that can be given to a preacher who visits the shul is that he is "talking through his *gatkes*."

The Simpleton

The Rebbe of Chutzp had a disciple—a simpleton. Not only did he not know his Alef-Beis, there were bad days when he couldn't even recall the Alef. But this simpleton could do one thing: He could play the flute very badly.

One day he came into the Beis Midrash, walked up to the Ark and said: "*Ribboyno shel Olyam*; I would like to davven *Minchah*, but I cannot read the, the, whatever it is. So, instead, I shall play you a tune on my flute."

With that he took out his flute and blew a piercingly bad note. Immediately a rain shower stopped, a cloud covered the face of the sun, the gates of heaven were closed, and a *Bat Kol* was heard saying "Aaargh!"

And all who heard had to agree.

The simpleton left Chutzp shortly afterwards and is now a famous chazan in New York.

The Rebbe and the Reform Shul

The Rebbe of Chutzp was nothing if not brave—
almost foolishly so, according to his (few) critics.
When he heard that a "Reform" shul had been established in a
neighboring town, he decided that such a disturbing development
demanded his immediate action. Calling for his second-best *streiml*

and his largest cloak (for he did not want to be recognized), he set forth to visit this den of impiety. He had heard how "churchy" the new heresy was so, walking with his head bowed low along the street (to avoid being seen), clutching his *tziszis* tightly under his cloak, and walking, by mistake, into Saint Stanislav's Cathedral, next door to the Reform temple, he was not at all surprised by what he saw when he raised his head and opened his eyes.

Awhile later he emerged, stunned and speechless. When he returned to Chutzp and had recovered, his Chasidim eagerly asked him for his opinion as to the new deviation. "Well," he said, "it's like this. I don't think we need to worry. For starters, the service seems to last for hours. It's led by a few fellows at the front, dressed in funny gowns. Almost no one else joins in at all. The whole thing is in a strange language—I didn't understand a word, and couldn't even find a spare book to follow. The service went on for hours, you couldn't hear half the things they were reading, and the fellow leading kiddush seemed to take ages. You even had to stand in line to get a sip! So I can't see any form of Judaism like that surviving, can you? Mind you," he added, "I did like the stained glass."

With that he went off to the Beis Midrash for *Maariv*.

The Meal Offering

In the little village of Einpferddorf, in the hills, was a small Jewish community numbering some 10 men and their families (mainly daughters). Enough, you might think, for a regular *minyan*, and such was indeed normally the case for the *Shachris* and *Maariv* services.

Alas, there was a problem—and the problem was that one of their number, Mottl, was the village baker. Such a baker! His breads and his cakes would melt in the mouth! But he worked at night, would always sleep in the day, and would not come to *Minchah*! Day after day, week after week, unless some stranger came to the village—a rare occurrence—there would be no *minyan* for *Minchah*. For *Shachris*, Mottl the Baker would come before going to bed; for *Maariv*, Mottl the Baker would get up in time before starting his work. As for *Minchah*—no way would he stir.

As time went by the other members of the little shul got increasingly angry. They would protest, they would argue—but Mottl stood firm. "Either you get your *minyan*-or you get your *mohnkuchen*," he would say. "Either you get to say Kaddish—or you get *challahs* for kiddush. Not both!" That was it.

The argument grew until one day, Yankel the *Shammas* thought to send a *shaylah* (question) to the Rebbe of Chutzp, to see if he could resolve the dispute. The Chutzper Rebbe thought long and hard, and eventually his *teshuvah* (response) was received with great excitement by the little *kehilah* (community). Yankel the Shammas opened it and began to read.

"On the one hand," the great sage began, "it is a custom sanctified since the time of our holy father Yitzchok that all Jews should

22

davven together at *Minchah* time. Did he not go out into the field in the afternoon to *davven?* On the other hand," he continued, "the *Minchah* prayer is descended from the afternoon service in the *Beis Mikdash,* as it says in *Vayikra, Parshas Tzav, 'Zos Towras ha-Minchah,'* referring to an offering of flour. Here we have a case where 10 men can be guaranteed for a *minyan* twice a day. Would that it were so in all our lands! At the third service, there are but nine who come. I have learned that it is the custom, in some places, in such a situation, to place a *Chumash* in the hands of a young boy and count him as the tenth—but as the citizens of Einpferddorf are blessed only with daughters, this too does not seem possible. Accordingly, I rule as follows:

"Since Mottl is a baker, it follows that he works with flour." At this, all those present gasped with admiration for the great man's learning. "Since, at the time of the *Minchah*, the Flour Offering, he is asleep, let him bring his *Minchah* at another time, when he is still awake. Let him bring to the synagogue every morning a sack of flour, to be distributed to the poor." At this both Yankel the *Shammas* and Nebbich Mendel became very excited, for they were the poorest of the community. "At the time of the *Minchah* prayers, if Mottl's sack is in Mottl's place, and a *Chumash* is spread before it, a *minyan* can be counted and the full service be said."

What joy spread through the village at the words of the Holy Chutzper Rebbe! The arrangement was accepted without further ado by everybody—even Mottl, who called it "half-baked" and added a kopeck to the price of every loaf from that day. Now, in the little village synagogue at *Minchah* time, Yankel the *Shammas* lifts Mottl's sack into his place while, in his other place, Mottl the Baker, himself, hits the sack.

The Journey to Lodz

It happened one winter's day that the Rebbe of Chutzp had to travel to Lodz on delicate business. He rose early in the morning, though not early enough, and went with his Chasidim to the station before saying the morning prayers. They were just in time for the train, and the Chasidim saw him into his compartment and wished him many greetings.

Just before the train departed, while the rebbe was still in the middle of *Tefillas ha-Derech*, a dark stranger threw the door open, hurled himself into the compartment, and sat, breathlessly, facing the rebbe. The rebbe didn't know the man and, tired, decided to stay silent.

The train set off, across the frozen countryside. *De-dum, de-dum, de-dum*...rattled the wheels of the carriage. Eventually the sun began to rise, and the sky turned from black to dark gray; it was time for *Shacharis*. The rebbe got down his bag, took out his *siddur*, his *tallis* and *tefillin*, and *davvened Shacharis*. Opposite him the stranger also arose, took out a *siddur* and *davvened*—but without *tallis* or *tefillin*! The rebbe listened carefully and—*gevalt!*—the stranger was *davvening* the *Maariv* prayers! "Aha!" thought the rebbe to himself, "perhaps this fellow is no *Yid*, but a police spy following me! He's pretending to be Jewish, but he's made a basic mistake. I won't trust him."

The train went on—*de-dum, de-dum, de-dum*—and the two men sat facing each other in silence. Eventually, after the sun had risen and had struggled as high as it ever was going to manage on this midwinter day, it was time for *Minchah*. The rebbe took out his *siddur*, and *davvened Minchah*. Opposite him, the stranger also took out a *siddur* and *davvened Minchah*. "Hmmm," thought the rebbe, "maybe this fellow is on the level after all. But then, if so, why that funny business this morning? I still don't trust him." So they sat, facing each other in silence, as the train struggled on—*de-dum, de-dum, de-dum....*

Though the journey was long, the afternoon was short, and soon it was dark again—time for *Maariv*. The rebbe took out his *siddur* and *davvened Maariv*. Opposite him, the stranger put on his *tallis* and *tefillin* and *davvened Shacharis!* The rebbe could hold himself back no longer.

"*Nu?*" he said. "Are you a *Yid* or are you a *Yid?*"

"I'm a *Yid*," said the stranger.

"So tell me, why have you *davvened* first *Maariv*, then *Minchah*, then *Shacharis*? Why have you *davvened* backwards all day?"

"*Nu?*" replied the stranger, "I've been traveling backwards all day, haven't I?"

A Branch of The Family

Reb Moshe of Chutzp had a beautiful daughter, Feigele. Every day she would stand at the little railway station that served the town and sell flowers to the travelers—such sweet flowers, each seeming to be blessed by the fair hand that held it. Few travelers could resist the charms of Feigele's blooms (though none was ever able to deflower her), and each day she brought back to her aged father enough money to support them.

Those of you who have been there will know, of course, that Chutzp is built on a hill and that the railway line that serves it is a branch line that curves up from the junction in the valley below. Each day the engine of the little train huffs and puffs its way up the curving lines, bringing the travelers from Lodz, from Cracow and from the whole wide world. One day, this little train brought with it the new porter, who worked at the Junction in the valley. He had transferred to Chutzp while Reb Berel was ill with the ague.

Avram—for this was the young man's name—and Feigele fell swiftly in love. During the long pauses between trains they would talk the sweet nothings that young people talk, and make plans for the future, for Avram was an expert in timetables. Both knew that when Reb Berel regained his strength and could cope once more with the trunks and the cases and the portmanteaux, Avram would be told to return once more to the valley and would no more be able to come up the winding branch line to see his beloved.

So, one evening, when finished with his duties for the day, but before the last train home was due to depart, Avram went to call on Reb Moshe, to ask for his daughter's hand in marriage. Reb Moshe received him well—he had heard good things of this helpful porter and admired his strong and healthy body—but refused to give his blessing. In vain did Avram plead, in vain did Feigele cry, in vain did even the neighbors, attracted by the noise, join in the debate and try to reason with him.

Reb Moshe was adamant. "I like the boy," he said, "and I am sure he is sincere, but one thing I promised to my dear Sarale before she passed away, and this promise I must keep. I cannot, and I will not, let my beautiful Feigele marry beneath her station!"

The Vusht

Tefillin For Two

The Randy Rebbe

The seventh Chutzper Rebbe is renowned for his book "*Goel Yedidi*," *The Dear Redeemer*. Indeed, it is from the title of this book that he is known as "*The Go Y*" or, in English, "*The Dear Re Me*."

In this work—an *aggadic* commentary on the halachic commentary of his grandfather, Reb Velvel Shem Tov ("The *VuSHT*"), on the semi-*aggadic* super commentary of the *Baalei Meshugoiim* on the marginal glosses of the Chelmsford edition of the *Midrash Brooklyn*—the *GoY* reveals how the Dear Redeemer of the Jewish People will come only when everyone, man or woman, wears *tefillin*, and everyone, man or woman, lights the *Shabbes* candles. These views—considered extreme in their time—led to the great controversy.

In a famous letter to the journal "*Divrei ha-Yamim Yehudi*," Reb Nosson of Derby (the *RaNDy Rebbe*) called attention to the implications, for Jewish psychotherapists, of having to *davven*, bound in leather straps, in the presence of women, and called upon the *GoY* to renounce his views. This the Chutzper Rebbe refused to do, and the correspondence in the journal (some of which has been translated and published in *The Jewish Chronicle Book of Amusing Letters to Place Upon Your Lavatory Window Ledge*) raged for many months.

Happily, the two *gedolim* were later reconciled and in later years spent many happy hours in the "Mrs. Cohen Twilight Home," drawing pictures for each other of exactly what each had meant. These drawings were destroyed afterwards by the Chutzper Chasidim.

Moshe Backwards

In the *shtetl* of Chutzp there lived an unfortunate man called Moshe, who was a cripple and weak of mind. He could not walk as does a normal man, but instead crawled sideways and backwards, like a crab. He was known in the *shtetl* as "Moshe Backwards." Further, he could not read and was unable to join in the prayers. Nevertheless, he would stand at the back of the Beis Midrash during the services, mumbling to himself in his own strange way.

One Yom Kippur, as all the Jews of Chutzp were praying, a feeling of oppression crept over them. All day they were fasting, beating their breasts, summoning all their reserves of *kavanah*—yet nothing seemed to avail. The atmosphere grew tense.

Suddenly, from the back of the shul, came scrabbling the bent figure of Moshe Backwards. As the congregation gaped, he climbed onto the *bimah*, turned (poor soul!) to the Holy Ark and, as the women in the gallery screamed and fainted, called out:

"*Ribboyno shel Oylam!* You have made me the way I am, so that I cannot even turn my head towards You without, *has v'chalilah*, turning my *tuchus* towards You at the same time. Yet I, Moshe, call upon You in the name of all the Jews of Chutzp for atonement and forgiveness!"

Immediately a miracle occurred! The shul trembled as a *bat kol* thundered forth: "By the name of Moshe Backwards shall I be worshipped here in Chutzp!" And ever since that wondrous day, the Jews of Chutzp have prayed from the Artscroll Siddur and have addressed God by the holy letters of Moshe's name—*Mem, Shin, Hey*—backwards!

The Lightning Bolt

Two Chasidim, a *chochom* (a wise one) and a *tam*, a *k'sil*, (a simple and innocent one) were walking in the forest and arguing. The *chochom* was a follower of Reb Berel Shinom, the "Rebish of Chutzp"; the *tam* was following the *chochom.* Despite this, they lost the path and soon the pair were lost in the forest. It began to rain, and a storm unleashed its fury over the forest.

Happily, they came to a large clearing, on the top of a hill, from where they were able to obtain a clear view over the surrounding countryside and the sky, in which lightning was beginning to flicker.

"Look!" said the *tam.* "It is light, it is beautiful, and with this light we can find our way home!"

"No," said the Chutzper Chasid; "it is a sign of *ha-Shem's* glory—let us stand here and gaze in awe!"

So they stood there together, in the clearing on top of the mountain, watching the lightning flash and flicker, ever closer towards them.

That is how they were found, two days later, still smoking gently.

Kosher Wine

One day, when the Rebbe of Chutzp had been studying Rashi on *halachos* (laws) of wine, he called his Chasidim together and told them: "It is a little-known fact that when the Children of Israel entered the Promised Land under Joshua, it was on a Sunday. (This is obvious, because they wouldn't have traveled on *Shabbes*, would they?) They decided, naturally enough, that on their first *Shabbes* in the Holy Land they would like to make a proper kiddush over the wine. But what could they use? In the desert, they had no vines, being nomads, a wandering people; even "Light Dessert" wine had not been possible. The wine of the Canaanites counted as "*Yayin Nesech*," (wine offered to idols) and was clearly forbidden. So what could they do?

Joshua therefore gave instructions that the Israelites should pluck the grapes from the laden vines. They did so. They then trampled the grapes, squeezing out the thick, red juice and pouring it into vats. Then they added sugar and boiled the juice until it was almost like treacle. Then they poured the juice into bottles.

Come the following Friday, *erev Shabbes*, the Israelites had sweet, thick red wine, all of five days old! A miracle! It is in memory of this miracle that, ever since that momentous Shabbes, the descendants of the Children of Israel celebrate all major festivals and events with *Carmel*, or *Kedem*, or *Manischewitz*, or *Thunderbird*.

The Holy Fish

One *Shabbes* afternoon, as the Rebbe of Chutzp was eating a tuna sandwich, he stopped and asked his Chasidim: "What is the special z'*chus* (merit) of this fish, that it deserves to be eaten by me?"

His Chasidim were puzzled and could make no reply.

"Well," he continued, "firstly, all fish have a special *z'chus* for the Jews, for from their earliest days they convene in schools. However, this tuna comes from the tunny fish. Don't say '*Tunny-fish*,' but '*Tun-nafesh*'—"be refreshed in your soul'—and that is why Tuna has the *z'chus* to be eaten on *Shabbes*."

Which explains why Chutzper Chasidim treasure this delicacy to this very day.

The Herring Aid

There are some who explain the Chutzper Rebbe's liking for fish by linking him to his famous first cousin, Reb Leib Meir of Pinsk. Reb Leib Meir used to enjoy pickled herring and once explained thus the secrets of his favorite delicacy:

41

"This herring is curled up tight—like the curved *shofar*, a sign of humility. Within it holds tightly a piece of onion—representing poverty, from the Hebrew '*Oni*'; it clasps also a piece of gherkin, to show that it is not embarrassed to welcome converts into its family, to have '*Ger*'kin. Finally, it is pickled in bitterness. Unlike herrings soused in wine, fit only for Chasidim likewise soused in wine, or herrings soused in schmaltsz, fit only for Chasidim soused in schmaltz, this herring symbolizes all that is so precious in our heritage."

In tribute to Reb Leib Meir of Pinsk his Chasidim named his favorite herring after him, and that is why it is called "The *Rollmop*" to this very day.

The Shabbes Lobbus

The fourth Chutzper Rebbe was so *frum* that he would not work at all on *Shabbes*—and this, he said, included his Rabbinical work. Soon after his return to Chutzp from the great Fallover Yeshivah, on the death of his saintly uncle, the third Chutzper Rebbe, he established the rule that the Jews of the town were allowed to *davven* only on the Holy Day. Non-Jews were employed to open the shul, to open the doors of the Ark, even to carry the scrolls! "If it's O.K. to have a *Shabbes Goy* at home," he would say, "then why not in shul as well?"

43

The rules grew stricter and stricter as the weeks passed. However, the day after the rebbe had announced that henceforth the pulling-up of breeches would also be classified as "work," as one of the 39 *melachos* (categories of forbidden labor), the elders of the congregation decided to take action. They went together to the rebbe's house and prevailed upon him, at first in vain, to relax these harsh restrictions, known to no other *kehilah* in the country. When it was pointed out to him that the money for all these "*Shabbes Goyim*" would have to come from the paltry funds collected for his own salary, he reluctantly conceded to the elders' pleadings. On one point, however, the rebbe remained adamant: Delivering sermons was, he said, very hard work, and as rabbi he could not allow this poor example to be set.

Accordingly, from that week on he arranged with the teacher of the local school to write introductions to each of the *sidras*—in Polish, of course, for being an intellectual who could read newspapers he knew no Yiddish—and to deliver them during the *Shabbes* morning service. Though few of the Jews could understand either the language or the subject matter, all agreed that he had a fine, dignified bearing and an expressive voice, and that no other shul in the country had sermons such as the ones he gave. After all, what else does a *kehilah* want from its sermons? The teacher became renowned throughout the locality. Even the rabbi would sit quietly through the sermons, his eyes closed to aid concentration, his breathing kept, he explained, deliberately deep and slow so as to enable him to use all his physical energies to absorb the messages of the *drasha*—messages that sometimes had such an effect on him that he felt himself rising to a higher world, from which he had to be shaken back when it was once more time for him to ascend the *bimah*.

All went well until one *Shabbes Chol ha-Moed Sukkos*; the rebbe had caught a slight chill the previous day while sitting in his neighbor's *sukkah*, and had had to treat it with several bottles of plum brandy at the home of the *gabbai*. In consequence, he was unable to attend the synagogue at all that *Shabbes* and had to content himself with praying from his bed. That day the teacher had the *bimah* to himself and let himself go.

For more than two-and-a-half hours he spoke on—well, no one could agree afterwards exactly what he had spoken about, though everyone agreed that, as usual, it had sounded very good. He spoke and he spoke. The time for the kiddush came and passed; the time for lunch came and passed. The women slipped from their places in the gallery to get the *chulent* out of the oven and place it on their tables in their *sukkahs*, where it grew cold and greasy. The time for *Minchah* came and passed. Still the preacher spoke on, with fiery eloquence, banging the lectern from time to time to jerk his listeners back to respectful attention.

Sukkos had been late that year, and the afternoons were already getting short. The *chazan* was getting frantic to continue the service, his stomach empty and his bladder full. Eventually the *shammas* had an idea and sent young Mottl to the rebbe's house with an urgent message.

Within ten minutes the rebbe, still tying his *gurtel*, walked into the shul and, casting his eyes around the weary congregation, mounted the *bimah* and whispered into the speaker's ear. With a curt nod the teacher stopped and walked to his seat, and the *chazan* began what became one of the shortest *Musaf* services in the history of Chutzp.

Afterwards the whole town was agog to learn what the rebbe had said, but he refused to disclose the contents of the message. The *shammas*, however, was more forthcoming. "I sent Mottl to the rebbe," he told his friends after the delayed *Minchah*, "to tell him to come quick." And I said to tell him, "If he didn't come quick, we'd ask him, the rebbe, to preach to us every *Shabbes*—because, after an hour, listening to the teacher was becoming work, and couldn't be allowed."

The Disputation

The wicked *galach* of Chutzp, the local priest, once challenged the Jewish community to a disputation, a debate about the rights and wrongs of his religion and the true one. After some worried discussion, the leaders of the community proposed that old Reb Berel should represent them, since he had once been, in his youth, a *shochet* in Warsaw and was therefore a Man of the World.

When the disputation started, it soon became clear that there were problems. For starters, Father Stanislav spoke no Yiddish. Secondly, Reb Berel, despite his five years in Warsaw, spoke no Polish at all.

After several hours the debate ended, with both sides claiming victory. For, as Father Stanislav said, "The Jews couldn't even answer our arguments," while, as Reb Berel said, "the *goyim* couldn't even understand our questions."

And, in fact, interfaith relations have remained at that same level in Chutzp to this very day.

The Niggun

All rebbes had their own *niggun*, their own wordless melody of devotion. The first Chutzper Rebbe used to sing this song to his Chasidim: "*Oy oy oy, oy oy oy, oy oy diddle-diddle-oy, oy, oy, oy!*"

Unfortunately, since he was tone-deaf, the melody was never preserved for us; however, we are assured on good authority that the angels in heaven used to cry on hearing him sing this *niggun*.

The Jester Who Stopped Laughing

O ld Yossl was a *tzachkan*—a clown, a Jester.
He made his living—huh, call that a living?—by making merriment at *simchahs*. No *simchah* in Chutzp was
complete without Old Yossl telling his jokes, poking fun at the
guests. For a bowl of borscht and a bottle of vodka, he would keep the
merriment going all evening. "*Yiddl mit dem Riddle*," they called
him.

As he got older, the fee went up to two bowls of borscht and two bottles of vodka. Unfortunately, he began to drink his fee even before the *simchah* began, so that, after a few years had passed, he no longer had even to put on a false red nose, since his own bulbous schnozzle was the right color already.

His material also began to change. For years he had taken as his motto "Stick to Yossl—the Old Jokes are the Best!" and guests would often know his stories by heart and join in his act, gaining more pleasure from telling the joke than listening to it. "Why did the chicken cross the road?" he would ask. "*Nu*, so why *shouldn't* the chicken cross the road, you got something against it?" he would answer himself, to howls of laughter. However, as the vodka took its toll, the nose got redder and the jokes got bluer.

But worse was to come for Yossl, for one day a new *tzachkan* came to town. Itzhik was a minstrel, a tumbler, a juggler. He could turn his hand to all sorts of party and card tricks. He was young, handsome and—for a jester—fairly sober. Suddenly, Old Yossl's bookings began to dry up—though he didn't—as the new man began to entertain the guests at *simchahs* with jokes that they hadn't even known existed. New jokes! New stories! Riddles with real answers! Punchlines! Poor Yossl could hardly compete.

The last straw was at the Shloimowitz *chassuneh* (wedding).

51

Miriam, the *kallah*, looked radiant, the rabbi hadn't made any mistakes (well, none of any importance), the feast was going well and then Old Yossl came lurching in, belched, and asked loudly, "So tell me—what's the difference between Miriam Shloimowitz and Zelda the *Zonah*?" There was a shocked silence, into which poured his answer: "Zelda's not so stupid as to marry her best customer!" The *klezmorim* tried valiantly to play over the gaffe, but the damage had been done, and Old Yossl was thrown out into the snow.

Bitter and angry, and more than a bit drunk, he began to scheme his revenge. Next Tuesday was to be Reb Fender's 70th birthday, and a banquet had been arranged. *Klezmorim* had been booked, there would be dancing for both the men and the women (though not together, of course!), and the minstrel had been engaged to warm up the party.

On the appointed evening, Old Yossl turned up, uninvited, and went to the rear of Reb Fender's mansion to the room where the players were preparing themselves. Itzhik, the warmer-upper, was warming himself up with a few somersaults and backward leaps on his mat. Yossl stepped forward and grunted. Surprised, Itzhik turned and saw his erstwhile competitor holding out his hand. Yossl said "Break a leg," the traditional greeting of players before a performance, and before Itzhik had time to pant out his thanks, Yossl pulled the mat away. Itzhik fell with a crunch.

The case made legal history. Reb Fender's widow sued Itzhik for letting Yossl take over and killing her husband with his attempts at humor. Yossl tried to claim his fee, saying that even though he hadn't been formally engaged, the host had died laughing. Itzhik tried to sue Yossl on grounds of Industrial Sabotage—and it was only through the skill of old Hirschel, the lawyer, that Yossl wasn't hanged. For this was the first time that a defense lawyer was able to successfully plead, on behalf of his client, that he was not fully responsible for his actions, because he suffered from *Pre-Minstrel Tension.*

The Pedestrian Zonah

In Lemberg there lived and worked a *zonah*—a prostitute—with a heart of gold. Her name was Sheyne, and for many years she used to help the young, unmarried yeshivah students in practical ways to understand the more complicated bits of Gemara—especially in tractates *Kiddushin* and *Nedarim*. (Married students from the famous *kollel* of Lemberg had to bring a signed note from the *rosh yeshivah* if they wanted to test the theories expounded in the minor tractate "*Kallah Rabbati.*")

So many students were helped by Sheyne that her fame spread among the graduates of the yeshivah, for her price was not beyond rubies, yet she was an *eshes choyil.* In vain did the Lemberger *maggid* inveigh against her, warning the *bochurim* that Aaron had died with a kiss on Mount Hor, or that "*Rodef Sholom*" meant to "pursue peace," not "pursue a piece." Her supporters outnumbered by far those who cursed her. (Indeed one such supporter immortalized her later when, writing a love song comparing his wife to his first educational experiences, he composed "*Bei Mir, Bist Du Sheyne.*")

Unlike many of her sisters, who sat in windows enticing men on their way from shul, Sheyne would walk up and down the pavements of the town looking for lonely clients to help. From this constant walking she came to be known as the "*Pedestrian Zonah,*" and there was even talk in the town council of erecting signs to that effect in the village center.

One Saturday evening in early June, as Sheyne strolled along her usual path, she met a stranger who was obviously not in a hurry to get to *Minchah.* Taking him back to her room, she prepared herself to provide her accustomed comforts and asked the stranger where he came from. "From Prague," came the reply. Immediately she jumped

from the bed, began to clothe herself, and urged the stranger to leave at once, "But why?" protested the innocent client. "Please leave," she urged again, "and come back in a couple of hours if you wish."
"What have I done wrong?" asked the puzzled man. "Nothing, nothing at all," she reassured him, "but you see, I have a duty to 'my boys,' and I cannot take a *Czech* on *Shabbes!*"

Torah Learning

T he Chutzper Rebbe told his disciples: "All learning is to be found in *Teyrah*, including pointless learning."

"How," asked his disciples, "could *pointless* learning exist in the *Holy Teyrah?*"

"Look and learn," said the rebbe. "The first word of the *Teyrah* is 'Bereshit.' The ordinary *chochom* will take these letters and see in them the beginning of all wisdom. But the *real chochom* will take these letters and rearrange them, the 'B,' the 'R,' the 'Sh,' the *Aleph* and *Yod* and make of it 'Rubbish'."

"True," said the most discerning of his disciples, "but what about the 'T'?"

"Ah yes," said the rebbe, "I quite forgot. With a *bissel* lemon, please, and two sugars."

A Mismatch

Reb Noggid of Chutzp had a daughter. Such a daughter! Her fish, her kugel, her pickles could melt in your mouth! Her hair—like shining jet. Her eyes—like jewels. As for the rest of her—well, perhaps it was best to concentrate on her fish, her kugel, her pickles and her eyes.

A follower of the rebbe, a humble student at the yeshivah of Chutzp, took meals at Reb Noggid's house every Thursday and fell deeply in love with her. What could he do, he a humble student? He went, naturally, to ask his master.

"Never!" exclaimed the rebbe. "Never—for this you came to Chutzp?" And he forbade him to see her again, muttering into his beard: "All the fine girls in town and my Chasid has to fall for a *Miss Noggid?*"

The Liar

Rachamim Shmuelevitz was an inveterate liar.
He couldn't even bring himself to say "Good
Morning" to anyone if the sun was shining. Three times he stood
under the *chuppah*, and each time he clearly did not mean to keep his
vows—after all, wasn't it Rachamim who, on that infamous occasion,
seduced the rebbetzin at the reception after his second wedding?

61

Not surprisingly, he had many enemies. The fact that he earned his living selling insurance policies hardly helped. The good folk of Chutzp soon learned the harsh lesson that the best policy was any policy so long as it wasn't *his* policy. Tiring of his occupation, Rachamim realized that he had to find a position where he could do what he wanted, when he wanted, say what he wanted, and not be held accountable. And so he entered politics and soon rose to prominence on the local town council. Here he was, at last, of great use to his fellow citizens, for they needed someone who could deal with the government at its own level, and Rachamim Shmuelevitz was the very man. Within ten years he had managed to convince the tsar's very own minister of finance that if income taxes were reduced to 85% on odd years he could always "get even" on even years; he then persuaded the then rebbe of Chutzp to declare the date on all official correspondence in the Russian date on odd years and in the Hebrew year on the other years so that there was never, apart from the odd months that fell between financial year-ends, an even number! In return for this concession he also persuaded the council of Chutzp to grant him the privilege of a monopoly in the assessment of all the town rates, and by the time of his untimely death he was unmourned by all.

On his tombstone are engraved the simple words: "Here Lies Shmuelevitz; As Usual."

Goldfinder and Dead Man's Gulch

There are many sad stories from the early days of Jewish settlement in America, and one of the saddest is the story of Boris Goldfinder.

The story really begins earlier, when Asher Wertvollstein and his wife Golda made the dangerous journey from Chutzp, via Memel and Liverpool, to Charleston (South Carolina) and settled there in the *Sephardi Kehilah*. Feeling, as the solitary *Ashkenazim*, rather unwanted and isolated, they moved with their young daughter to Savannah, where Wertvollstein changed the family name to Worthingstone and built up a thriving business in cotton and gin through his links with the famous "cotton gins" of Lancashire.

Boris came a little later to the *Goldeneh Medineh*—with the trekkers of '45—and when he had made his fortune, he settled in Onehorseville, Wyoming. There he opened a dry goods store and made his second fortune, since his was the only shop in Onehorseville that sold anything that was dry. Soon his attention turned to thoughts of marriage—but where was he, a loner from *der heym*, to find a wife, especially one of good *Ashkenazi* stock? Like many a lonely man before him, he decided to write to a *shadchan*.

Meanwhile, the Worthingstones were thinking of finding a husband for their lovely daughter Hannah—and not just *any* husband, but a fine, upstanding *Ashkenazi* husband. They, too, decided to write to the Matrimonial Agency run by Miss Pearl Neckliss in New York.

Matters took their course, and eventually the lonely, rich Boris received a charming letter, and an even more charming portrait, from a southern state. Eagerly he responded, and before long a meeting was arranged. Here there was a problem. There was no way Boris could afford to close up his shop for the time needed to travel to the coast and back, and Asher and Golda were getting a little too old—and too fond of the gin—to travel well. So, with some forebodings, it was agreed that Hannah would travel on her own, but that Boris would (of course!) arrange for her to be put up at the town's best hotel.

Then came further snags. How could she travel? The railroad stretched westwards across the plains, but from Dodge City there was a stagecoach only twice a week. The Friday one was out—for, of course, she would not arrive until after *Shabbes* has begun; so it would have to be the Tuesday one.

At last everything seemed settled and sealed and then—disaster! Poor Boris discovered, to his dismay, that the Tuesday stagecoach did not travel direct to Onehorseville, but made a detour en route to serve the mining settlement of Dead Man's Gulch, to deliver the weekly supplies of whisky, ammunition and coffin handles! Desperately he sent an urgent message by the fastest Pony Express—but it came too late.

Hannele, poor beautiful Hannele, never arrived at Onehorseville. On the way she was made an offer she couldn't refuse; she got off at

Dead Man's Gulch and made for herself a career of the sort that respectable people don't talk about. She was tough as old nails and became infamous as "Hard-hearted Hannah, the Vamp from Savannah."

As for Boris, he died of a broken heart, for there wasn't another *Ashkenazi* bride within a thousand miles. It is said that, if you stand around the Greyhound Terminal in Dodge City late at night you can still hear his spirit wandering around, crying plaintively into the darkness, "Don't put your daughter on the stage, Mrs. Worthingstone!"

GLOSSARY OF TERMS

Please note: Most Hebrew and Yiddish terms are hard to convey in English letters, since certain vowels or consonants, and the stresses within words, are not the same in the different languages. In addition, some of the humor in these tales depends on presenting characters as though they had specific accents with connotations of "backwoods" or parochial East-European attitudes, so that the words may be spelled differently from how they would appear in scholarly dictionaries.

Apikoros/Epikoros (Greek): One dedicated to physical rather than spiritual pleasures. A term of denigration used by fundamentalists of intellectuals.

Beis ha-Medrash/Beis Midrash (Yiddish): lit. house of study; a term used for synagogue.

Bet Din: A religious court, Rabbinic court, set up to decide on matters of Jewish status, marriage and divorce, adoption, etc., and to adjudicate as required on other disputes.

Betzim (Hebrew): Eggs. (Used as a euphemism for testicles.)

Bimah: Pulpit, raised platform from which the synagogue service is led.

Chabad: Acronym used by Lubavitch Chasidim.

Chag, Chagim: Festivals.

Chasid: A semi-mystical movement originating in Eastern Europe in the 18th century, that soon divided into groups known usually by the town of their origin (e.g., Satmar, Lubavitch, Bobov, Bratslav). Of these the Lubavitch movement is now the most widely known due to its policy of outreach to the wider community and its messianic beliefs; other groups prefer a more inward approach, and there are major theological disagreements among the different schools, representing the teachings of their

Chassuneh: (Yiddish): A wedding.

Chatan: Bridegroom

Chazan: Cantor, one who leads the service by chanting musically.

Chelm: A real town in Poland, used as the location for a series of original Yiddish humorous stories poking fun at its townspeople's excessive naivety. "Chelmsford" is a real English town (in Essex) and is used here as a pun on "Chelm."

Chulent: A slow-cooked hot stew (ingredients vary) eaten on the Sabbath. Since cooking is not allowed on the Sabbath, chulent is started ahead of time.

Chutzp: A fictional town, but by turning this fictional noun into a fictional adjective "Chutzper" (as in "the rebbe of Chutzp" = "The Chutzper Rebbe") a verbal pun is made with the term "Chutzpah," Hebrew and Yiddish for "outrageous cheek."

Davven (Yiddish): Pray, worship.

Der Heym (Yiddish): The homeland, i.e., Eastern Europe.

Drasha: Exegetical homily on a text.

Erev: Evening.

Erev Shabbes: The Sabbath evening (Friday night).

Frum: Pious (usually over-pious).

Gabbai: Financial administrator of a synagogue.

Galach (lit): "Shaven one." A Christian priest (presumably tonsured).

Ganeff/Goneff (Yiddish): Thief.

Gatkes: A Yiddish phrase for thermal underwear.

Gematria: Scheme for calculating mystic meanings from the numerical equivalents of the letters of the Hebrew alphabet.

Ger (Hebrew): Stranger, outsider. Used also to mean a convert to Judaism, i.e., one who has come in from outside.

Giyur: Conversion—the process.

Goldeneh Medineh (Yiddish) lit: "Golden Country." Term used for America by those longing to emigrate there.

Gurtel: A belt used symbolically to mark off the lower half of the body.

Haftarah: Readings from the Prophets on Sabbaths and festivals.

Hagbahah: Elevation of the Scroll of the Law.

Havdalah: Ceremony to mark the end of the Sabbath.

Kallah: Bride.

Kehilah (Hebrew): Community.

Ketubah: Marriage contract document.

Kiddush: lit. Sanctification. Blessing over wine.

Klezmer, Klezmorim (Yiddish): Musicians.

Kosher (Hebrew—*Kasher*): Fit. e.g., food fit to eat; a scroll, a prayer book—fit to use.

Kotel (Hebrew): Term for the Western Wall of the Temple in Jerusalem.

Litvak: A Lithuanian or one of Lithuanian descent.

Lobbus (Yiddish): Oaf.

69

Maariv: Evening service.

Maftir: Concluding section of the weekly Torah reading.

Mashiach (Hebrew): Messiah.

Mikveh: A ritual bath; immersion in a mikveh is part of the process of conversion (though it is not the same as "baptism" with which it is frequently confused) and is also part of the process of spiritual purification after contact with blood (whether menstrual or through violence, a corpse, or other ritual defilement).

Minchah: Afternoon service. In the Bible it also referred to a flour-offering sacrifice in the Temple.

Minyan: Quorum of 10 adult males required before certain prayers can be recited; defined as the minimum size of a "community" for communal prayers and readings.

Misnaged: An opponent of Chasidism.

Mohel: Ritual circumciser.

Mohnkuchen: Poppy-seed cakes.

Musaf: Additional service (on Sabbaths and festivals).

Reb: Yiddish for "Mister." Courtesy title, implying no specific powers.

Rebbe: Yiddish term for rabbi—but meaning also a teacher with additional spiritual powers, as opposed to a rabbi, whose title implies only judicial and educational powers within a community. A rebbe is the spiritual head of a "movement" or a "school" within Chasidic Judaism.

Rebbetzin: Rabbi's wife.

Shabbes: Sabbath.

Shabbes Clock: Device for turning electrical appliances on or off on the Sabbath by pre-setting the mechanism.

Shabbes Goy: A non-Jew employed to perform work on the Sabbath that Jews are not permitted to do—e.g., lighting fires.

Shacharis: Morning service

Shaliach Tzibbur (Hebrew): Representative of the congregation, i.e., the person who leads the prayers on behalf of the rest of those attending a service.

Shammas: Synagogue caretaker/warden/guardian.

Sheitel (Yiddish): Wig worn by married women.

Sheva Brochos: The seven blessings recited for a newly married couple.

Shivah: Week of initial mourning after a bereavement.

Shlemiel: Idiot, innocent fool.

Shochet: A ritual slaughterer, charged with slaughtering animals for consumption as kosher meat and with ensuring that the animal is healthy and the process is swift and painless, carried out with respect and sensitivity to the animal.

Shtetl (Yiddish): Small town or village.

Shul (Yiddish): School—term used for synagogue

Siddur: Prayer book.

Simchah: A joyful occasion, family or communal celebration.

Streiml: Fur hat or a type worn by Chasidim.

Taharas ha-Mishpochah: Family purity laws.

Tallis: Prayer shawl worn at morning services.

Tashlich: Ceremony at New Year when sins are symbolically "cast into the waters."

Tefillin: Phylacteries—small boxes containing scriptural verses worn strapped to the head and arm during weekday morning services.

Tichel (Yiddish): Headscarf worn by women.

Torah/Teyrah: The First Five Books of the Hebrew Scriptures; also used as a term for the entire Hebrew Bible and for all forms of learning.

Tzitzis: Fringes on prayer shawl. Worn by some all day under their outer clothing.

Yayin Nesech: Wine that has (possibly) been offered or poured out to pagan idols and therefore unsuitable for consumption by Jews; the term sometimes used for any wine whose kosher provenance cannot be guaranteed.

Yeshivah: Academy for study of religious texts.

Z'chus, Z'chut (Hebrew): Merit.

Zonah (Hebrew/Yiddish): Whore, harlot, prostitute.

Other titles from Alef Design Group

For Adults

STORIES AND ESSAYS ABOUT GENDER
AND JEWISH SPIRITUALITY

Joel Lurie Grishaver

The Alef Design Group

The Bonding of Isaac

Joel Lurie Grishaver

Issues of gender and spirituality are the subject of the new work by Joel Lurie Grishaver. Weaving together traditional Jewish texts with books, movies and other elements of popular culture, Mr. Grishaver considers the way men and women approach their own spiritual and relationship needs.

Is there another writer and thinker in the Jewish community like Joel Grishaver? I think not. This book is Grishaver unbound: wit, wisdom, lore, learning, midrash and memoir—the full range of his genius playing with and pondering core texts, core issues, bringing the Torah vitally alive. The Bonding of Isaac *is both in form and in content a unique book. Bravo, brother!*—Peter Pitzele, author of *Our Father's Wells*

Hardcover • Gender/Spirituality • ISBN #1-881283-20-8 • $21.95

1994-1995 TORAH ANNUAL
A COLLECTION OF THE YEAR'S BEST TORAH

Learn Torah With... 5755 Torah Annual

A Collection of the Year's Best Torah

Joel Lurie Grishaver & Rabbi Stuart Kelman, editors

In the traditional Jewish library there is a collection of volumes known as the Commentators' Bible. In it, arranged by weekly Torah portion, insights created over hundreds of years and in dozens of countries. Diversity has always been the key to Jewish learning.

Learn Torah With... was a weekly electronic dialogue on Torah featuring over a hundred great Torah teachers of all ideologies and disciplines from all over the world. Their comments and thoughts on the *parashot* are meshed with the insights and observations of dozens of the thousands who subscribed to this electronic conversation. This new "American-Style" Jewish Commentators' Bible has been edited and collated out of that conversation.

September 1996 • 450 pages • Hardcover • Adult • Torah • ISBN #1-881283-13-5 • $28.95

73

The Kosher Pig
And Other Curiosities of Modern Jewish Life
Rabbi Richard Israel/illustrations by Shan Wells

Richard Israel has been the only rabbi in Bombay, India, a beekeeper, a success-ful marathon runner, and the director of Hillel Jewish Student Centers on vari-ous college campuses. These diverse experiences give him a unique vantage point on the chaos which is modern Jewish life. He gets caught in the tension between being a traditional Jew and being a modern American...and suspects that, indeed, he may be neither.

Softcover • Jewish Life • ISBN #1-881283-15-1 • $14.95

40 Things You Can Do to Save the Jewish People
SOME REALLY PRACTICAL IDEAS FOR PARENTS WHO WANT TO RAISE "GOOD ENOUGH" JEWISH KIDS TO INSURE THAT THE JEWISH PEOPLE LAST AT LEAST ANOTHER GENERATION
Joel Lurie Grishaver

An insightful book on Jewish parenting by a middle-aged divorced man without children, *40 Things* is based on the many failures and few successes of the author's friends' attempts to be perfect Jewish parents. It is a practical book about improving the odds which asks: "How much can we get away with and still raise fully Jewish children who will in turn raise other Jewish children?"

Softcover • Parenting/Education • ISBN #1-881283-04-6 • $16.95

Eight Great Dreidel Stories
Martin Gal

Hanukkah is not just for children. Every year Martin Gal writes a new Hanukkah story. Each year, he mails them to his friends as presents. The stories have noth-ing in common except that somewhere in each plot is a dreidel. These stories are for you to enjoy after the kids have gone to bed, or have grown up and left home. You deserve a present, too. These stories are the kind of Hanukkah sto-ries they don't teach in Hebrew School.

Softcover • Hanukkah • ISBN #1-881283-10-0 • $13.95

Being a Blessing:
54 Ways You Can Help People Living with AIDS
Rabbi Harris R. Goldstein

This amazingly simple book by Rabbi Harris R. Goldstein leads us through the understanding and the actions needed to live up to the best of our intentions. Things as varied as "AIDS 101," how to visit a person living with AIDS, "people with AIDS Bill of Rights," and what it means to be created in God's image. The educational, the religious and the political aspects of the AIDS crisis are included—basic information on how to be a good person at a scary time.

Softcover • AIDS • ISBN #1-881283-08-9 • $13.95

Soul Stories and Steps
Trudy Ettelson, Ph.D.

Jews have a long tradition of weaving their own stories between the line of the Biblical text. This embroidery of the Bible is called Midrash. In this collection of original stories, Trudy Ettelson weaves her own understanding of the Jewish tradition, not only around the Biblical text, but around the 12 Steps as well. Here is a spiritual book steeped in Jewish tradition, leading one along a path toward recovery.

Softcover • Spirituality • ISBN #1-881283-07-0 • $6.95

For Families

Stark's Amazing Jewish Family Cookbook

Written and Illustrated by Mark Stark

This cookbook is a collection of secret family recipes and a celebration of Jewish cooking. Everything is ready for even the most beginning cook—hand-drawn recipes show the ingredients, the tools needed, and the steps used to make them. Recipes are listed by holiday, with a description of the holiday's celebration. All recipes are coded for adherence to kashrut, the religious and dietary laws of the Jewish people. For those who want to discover the fun of creative Jewish cooking, this book is a must.

Softcover • Family • Cooking/Jewish Life • ISBN #1-881283-19-4 • $26.50

Eight Nights, Eight Lights

Rabbi Kerry M. Olitzky

Courage. Gratitude. Sharing. Knowledge. Service. Understanding. Love. Hope. Eight nights. Eight lights. Eight family values. In this joyous and reflective work, Rabbi Kerry M. Olitzky provides families with a way of letting their Hanukkah celebrations affirm not only their Jewish identity, but the very Jewish values they wish to transmit to their children.

Softcover • Family/Hanukkah • ISBN #1-881283-09-7 • $8.95

For Children

Let's Talk About the Sabbath

Dorothy K. Kripke/Illustrated by Joy Nelkin Weider

Off the pen of a well-respected children's author, *Let's Talk About the Sabbath* is a young person's guide to the Sabbath. From meeting the Queen of the Sabbath, to celebrating Havdallah, this book delights in the visions of a perfect Sabbath experience. Ms. Kripke enchants readers with all the aspects of Sabbath, including candles and wine, Sabbath angels, study and prayer, Sabbath joy, and the farewell to this special day. The full-color illustrations by Joy Nelkin Weider direct the eye to the beauty of the Sabbath.

Hardcover • Middle Reader • The Shabbat • ISBN # 1-881283-18-6 • $16.95.

Sing Time

Bruce H. Siegel/Illustrated by Joshua Siegel

A ten-year-old "master of the fast comeback" and connoisseur of rock and roll discovers in half an hour how a single teacher, a Cantor, can impact his life. This Cantor doesn't just sing songs, he shares the value of a single moment in time, and how music is the "calendar" of Jewish life. Cantor Jacobs steers our hero down a path he might never have taken otherwise, all because his dad decided that Jerry-the-Jerk (his older brother, Gerald) should have a bar mitzvah.

Softcover • Middle Reader • Jewish Connections • ISBN # 1-881283-14-3 • $5.95

Champion & Jewboy: TWO NOVELLAS

Bruce H. Siegel/Illustrated by Spark

Two young adult novellas by Bruce H. Siegel are bound together in *Champion & Jewboy*. The first novella, *Champion*, follows a young boys discovery of his grandfather's hidden past as a boxer. The story reveals the anti-Semitic treatment the grandfather received in Germany as he tried to become an Olympic boxer.

The second novella, *Jewboy*, features a teenager convicted of vandalizing a synagogue who is transported through time to witness and participate in the most famous anti-Semitic event of the 20th century.

Softcover • Young Adult • Self-Discovery • ISBN #1-881283-11-9 • $6.95

The Swastika on the Synagogue Door

J. Leonard Romm/illustrated by Spark

When a suburban synagogue on Long Island is attacked by anti-Semitic vandals, the hatred manifest in the spray paint forces the Lazarus kids to confront their own history, their own prejudice, and still find the guilty party.

This mystery for young adult readers takes them on an exciting roller-coaster through Jewish history and contemporary Jewish reality. The surprise ending is bound to get you, too.

Softcover • Young Adult • Anti-Semitism • ISBN #1-881283-05-4 • $6.95

The Grey Striped Shirt

Jacqueline Jules/Illustrated by Mike Cressy

Frannie is looking for Grandma's purple hat with the feather. By accident she discovers a grey striped shirt with a yellow star hidden in the back of the closet. Slowly, she begins asking her Grandparents questions. Slowly they begin to unfold the story of their Holocaust experience. This novel for middle readers gently reveals the truths about the Holocaust without reducing it to a horror show.

Softcover • Middle Reader • Holocaust • ISBN #1-881283-21-6 • $8.50

Dear Hope... Love, Grandma

Hilda Abramson Hurwitz & Hope R. Wasburn, Edited by Mara H. Wasburn

Eight-year-old Hope had a school project to become the summer pen pal of a senior citizen. When her assigned pen pal failed to write back, her mother suggested she write to her grandmother. A two-year correspondence resulted.

This book is a collection of letters in which Grandma reveals the stories of her childhood, the difficulties growing up in turn-of-the-century St. Louis, and some wonderful and joyous insights about human hearts.

Hardcover • Middle Reader • Autobiography • ISBN #1-881283-03-8 • $13.95

Tanta Teva and the Magic Booth

Joel Lurie Grishaver/Illustrated by David Bleicher

It all started when Marc (with a "C") Zeiger ran away one night to get his parents to buy him a Virtual Reality hook-up (it's a long story). In the dark, lost in a part of the woods which couldn't possibly exist, he encounters Tanta Teva, a cleaning lady who is busy scrubbing graffiti off rocks in the forest. Together they visit young Joshua, David and Hillel. When Marc returns home, no one really believes the stories of where he'd been and who he'd met!

Softcover • Middle Reader • Fantasy • ISBN #1-881283-00-3 • $5.95

A Mouse in Our Jewish House

Florence Zeldin/Illustrated by Lisa Rauchwerger

This imaginative counting book by noted children's author Florence Zeldin combines the mastery of counting from one to twelve with the introduction of the basic celebrations of the Jewish year. A mouse named Archie Akhbar inhabits this book. Brought to life by the imaginative paper sculptures of Lisa Rauchwerger, Archie eats an escalating number of pieces of food on each subsequent Jewish holiday.

Hardcover • Picture Book • Jewish Holidays • ISBN #0-933873-43-3 • $11.95

A Sense of Shabbat

A Sense of Shabbat

Faige Kobre

In the sensuous photographs and simple text that make up this picture book, the taste, feel, sound, look and touch of the Jewish Sabbath all come alive. The Sabbath presented here is at once holy and wondrous, comfortable and familiar.

Hardcover • Picture Book • Sabbath • ISBN #0-933873-44-1 • $11.95

Order Information

_____ Learn Torah With…5755 Torah Annual (hc) $28.95 ...._____

_____ The Bonding of Isaac (hc) $21.95 ...._____

_____ Tales of the Chutzper Rebbe (hc) $16.50 ...._____

_____ The Kosher Pig (pbk) $14.95 ...._____

_____ 40 Things You Can Do to Save the Jewish People (pbk) $16.95 ...._____

_____ Eight Great Dreidle Stories (pbk) $13.95 ...._____

_____ Being A Blessing (pbk) $13.95 ...._____

_____ Soul Stories and Steps (pbk) $6.95 ...._____

_____ Stark's Amazing Jewish Family Cookbook (pbk) $26.50 ...._____

_____ Eight Nights, Eight Lights (pbk) $8.95 ...._____

_____ Let's Talk About the Sabbath (hc) $16.95 ...._____

_____ Sing Time (pbk) $5.95 ...._____

_____ Champion/Jewboy (pbk) $6.95 ...._____

_____ The Swastika on the Synagogue Door (pbk) $6.95 ...._____

over

_____	The Grey Striped Shirt (pbk) $8.50´.. _____
_____	Dear Hope...Love, Grandma (hc) $13.95.. _____
_____	Tanta Teva and the Magic Booth (pbk) $5.95 .... _____
_____	A Mouse in the Jewish House (hc) $11.95 .... _____
_____	A Sense of Shabbat (hc) $11.95 .... _____

Shipping & Handling—$5.50 for the first book, $2.00 each additional book....... _____

California residents: Please add 8.25% sales tax... _____

Total.. _____

Name _____

Address _____

_____

City _____

State _____

Zip _____

A check is enclosed for _____

Charge to my credit card:
  � VISA   � MASTERCARD   � AMEX

Name on card_____

Card # _____

Expiration Date_____

Alef Design Group

4423 Fruitland Avenue, Los Angeles, CA 90058
800-845-0662 • 213-582-1200
fax: 213-585-0327 • e-mail: <misrad@torahaura.com>